To Luna,
  Enjoy the memories
you make today, and
everyday, in the park!

A Little Park Publishing

This book is dedicated to my Papa, Dr. Alton Little. Thank you for teaching me how to be inspired by all the possibilities a park holds, and the impactful ways they shape our communities for the better. You were the greatest park and recreation professional this world has ever known, and I was just blessed to also call you Papa.

One of my favorite places in the entire world to go is to the park! My family and I often spend time at the park, just like we are going to today.

Today, my family brought a picnic lunch to enjoy. We like to find a large shade tree to sit under when we visit the park.

Luckily, this park has plenty of trees to choose from!

After enjoying our picnic, it's time to play! I like to fly kites in the park or look for bugs. What do you like to do in the park?

Many people visit the park just like my family. Today, I see an older man sitting by himself on a park bench, so I decide to talk to him.

"Sir, are you enjoying the park today?" I ask.

"Why, yes I am! I love to visit the park. It feels like home," he says.

"I do too! It's my favorite thing to do!" I say excitedly.

"Tell me, if you could build your perfect park, what all would it have in it?" the man asks

I began to dream of all the things I would want in my perfect park...

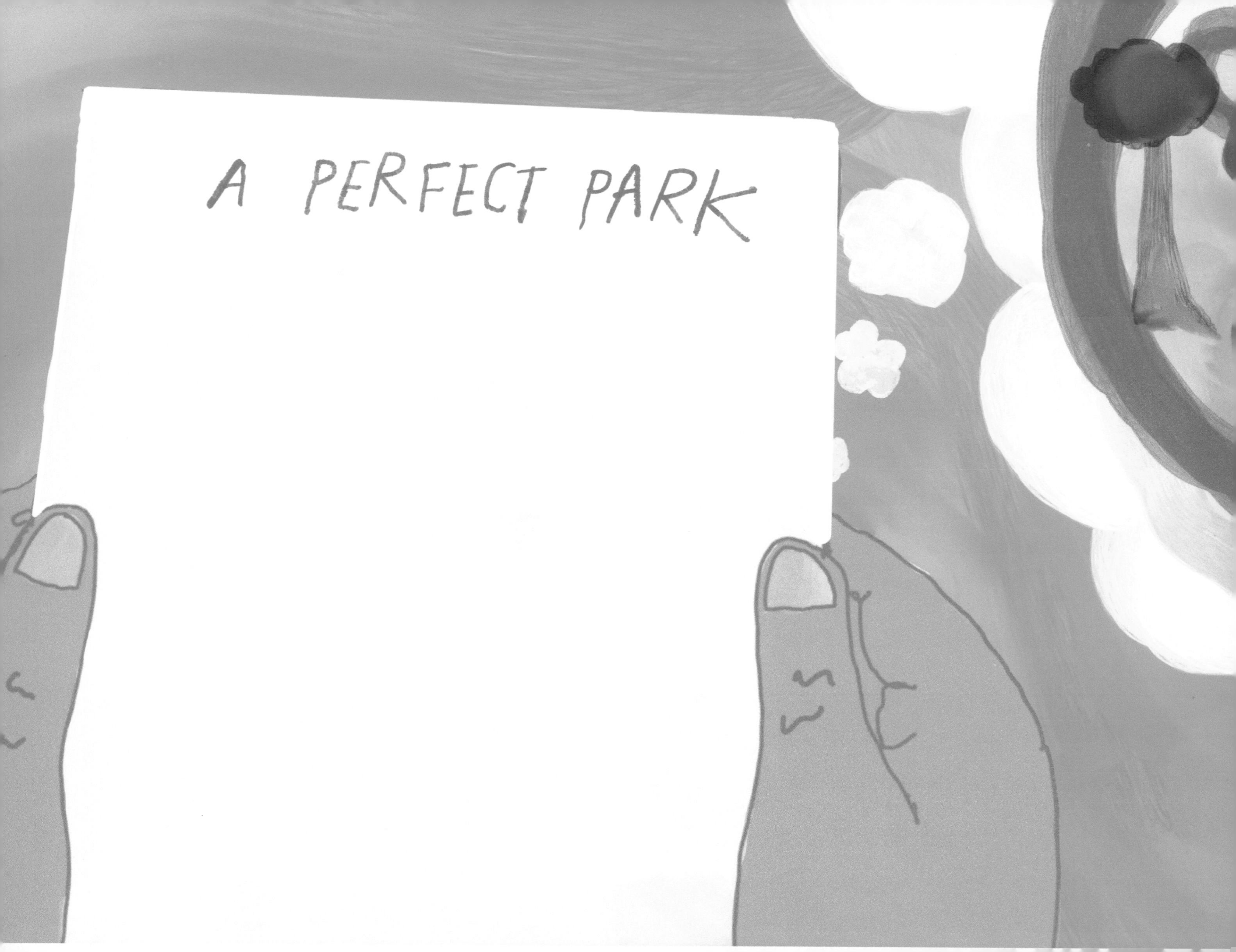
A PERFECT PARK

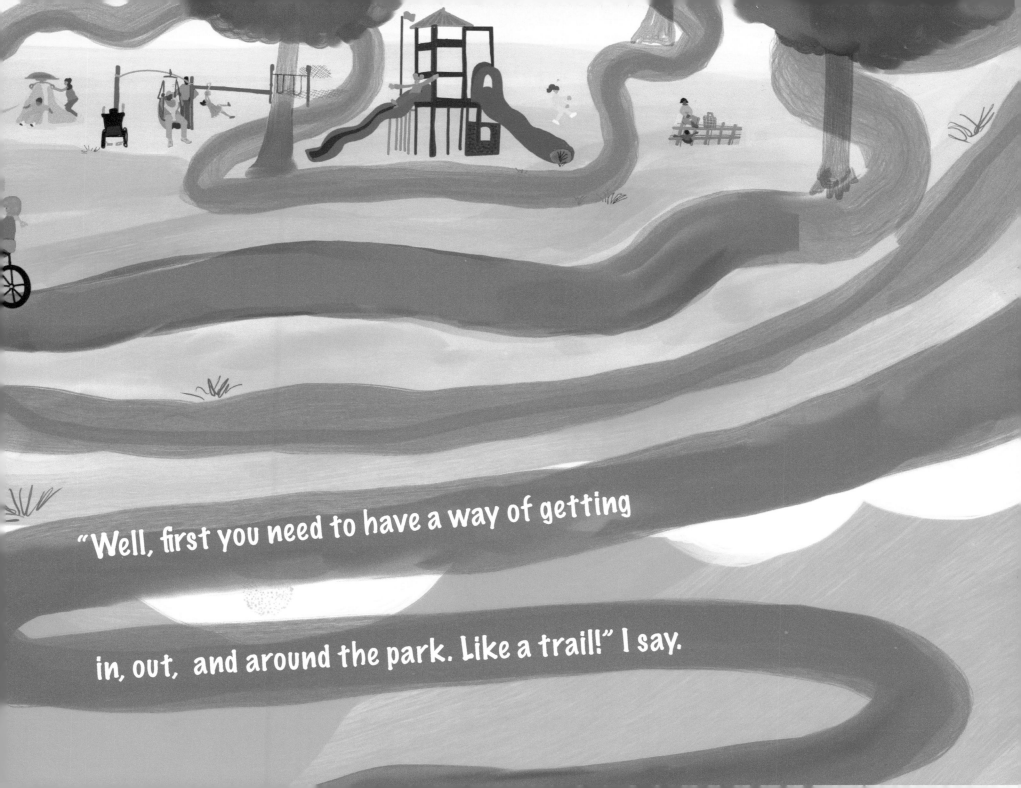

"Well, first you need to have a way of getting in, out, and around the park. Like a trail!" I say.

"Sometimes when I walk through a park on a trail, I like to imagine I am walking with dinosaurs in a forest!"

"I also would have lots and lots of trees in my park."

"The more trees, the more picnics!
My family enjoys picnics in the park, so I know
others would enjoy them too!"

"Oh, and I want to fish in my park!
I would add a dock near the pond.
Fishing is something I love doing
with my grandpa!" I say to the man.

"One time when I was fishing, I caught a fish the size of a big whale! Maybe some of those fish will be in my park, too?!"

"My perfect park would also have the biggest, most ginormous playground EVER!" I say using my arms to show the size.

"A playground is the heart of any park!" The man says with a smile.

"Sometimes, I like to imagine the playground as a big pirate ship!"

"Where I can...slide from one side of the ship to the other..."

"...and glide over the water to avoid the hungry crocodiles..."

"Then, everyone on the ship will celebrate with singing and dancing because we found the treasure!"

"Your park is sounding like quite the amazing place! Is there anything else you would include in your perfect park?" the man asks.

"Well, I do love sports. I think I would like to have a place for baseball in my park..."

"...and imagine myself up to bat, bases loaded in the bottom of the 9th. I would hit a grand slam every time in my park!"

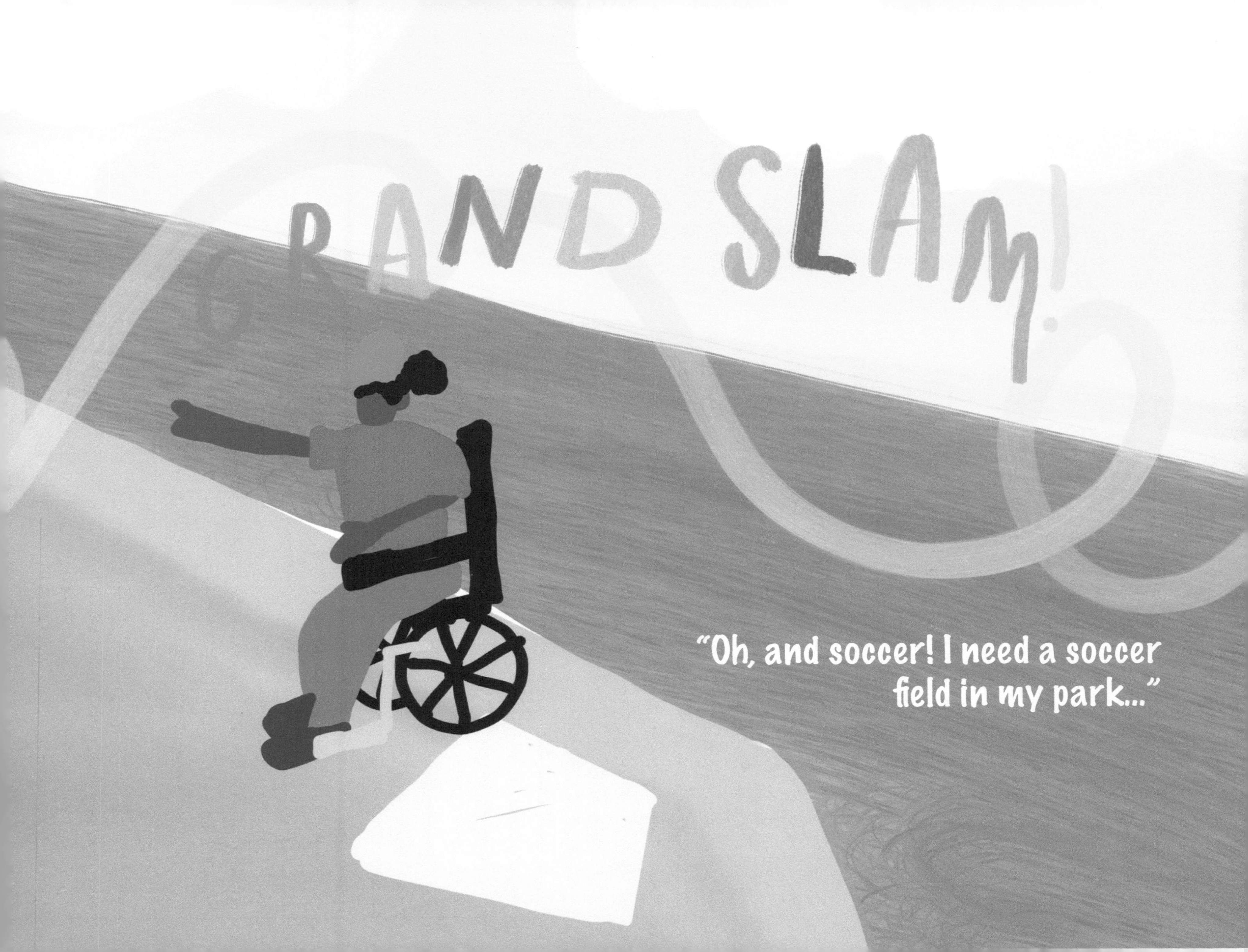

"Oh, and soccer! I need a soccer field in my park..."

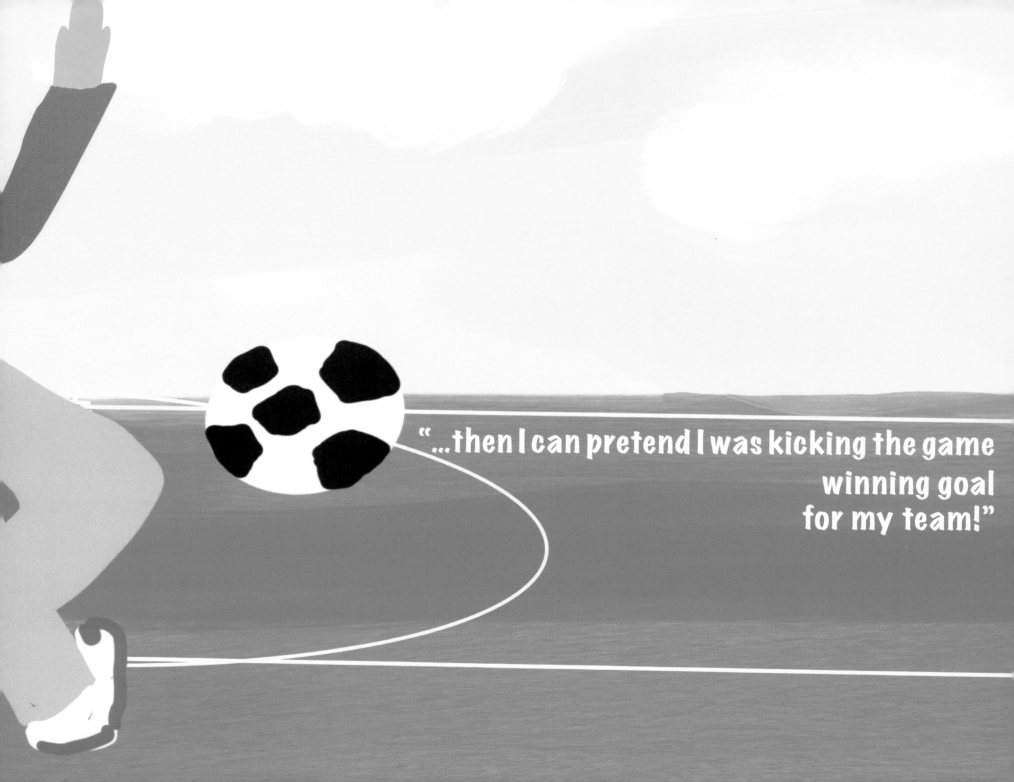

"I also love to play basketball, so I would add a court to my park!"

HERE COMES THE HOME TEAM!

"I like playing basketball with my grandma. She acts like the announcer and says,

"Here comes the home team!"

as I run onto the court."

"Do you have any pets?" the man asks.
"I do! I have two dogs", I say.
"Maybe they need to have a place to play at the park, too..." the man responds.

"You're right! Dogs can have their own space to rule like a castle! They can run around their kingdom in circles until they get dizzy!"

"My friends and I like to ride different things with wheels too. A place to do that would be cool!

Some of my friends like to ride their bikes, and some like to skateboard. I like to ride my scooter."

"I think one day, I can try to do the big-ramp
like the pros! But for now,
I will just stick to flat ground..."

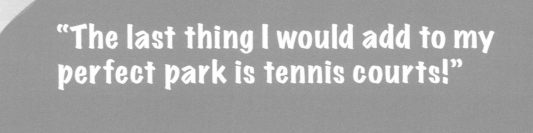

"The last thing I would add to my perfect park is tennis courts!"

"I like to play tennis with all my friends. Everyone can play, and we can play together!"

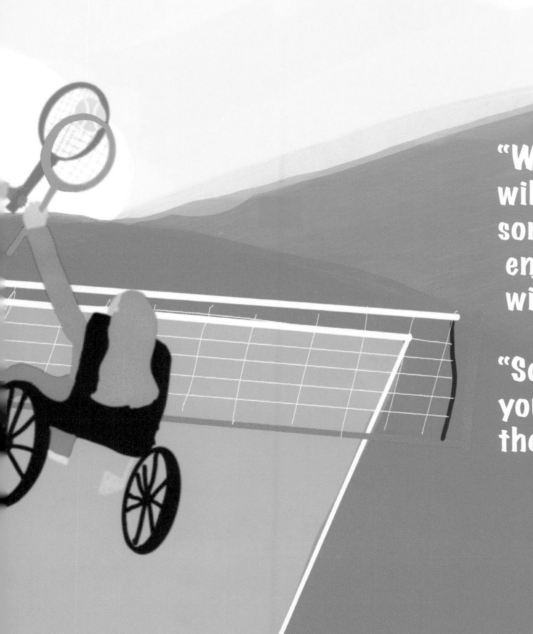

"Wow, it sounds like your park will have a little something for everyone to enjoy!" the man says with excitement.

"So what would you include in your perfect park, sir?" I ask the man

"You see, play is all you imagine it to be, and a park is like your blank canvas. But I want you to remember one thing," he says.

"What's that, sir?" I ask.
"It's not the things in the park that make it special, it's all the people that will enjoy using it that make it perfect." the man says with a twinkle in his eye.